Dear Little Brown Girl:

My Travels Around the World

WRITTEN AND ILLUSTRATED BY: SHENEKA BROWN, M. ED

Dear Little Brown Girl: My Travels Around the World

Published by Inspire One Success Academy, Inc.
Text Copyright © 2018 by Sheneka Brown.
Illustration copyright © 2018 by Sheneka Brown.

https://www.dearlittlebrowngirl.org

ISBN-13: 978-0692082034
ISBN-10: 0692082034

Description:
Chloe wants to go outside and play; however, it's a rainy day. She stays in the house to read; only to find herself in a dream. In her dream, she travels the world and learn about the culture, language, and history of many countries across the globe.

Genre:
Realistic Fiction

<u>Dedication</u>

This book is dedicated to Josiah, Jordan, Nicholas, Camille, Corey, Gabby, Kimberly, Akiyah and Aniyah. It is also dedicated to every little boy or girl who has a dream.

It was a rainy Saturday morning. The clouds were gray and a storm was coming near. It was too wet and dangerous to go outside and play.

"Chloe, come downstairs and play games with us," yelled her Mom from downstairs.

"It's okay, Mom! I think I will just read a book. After I finish reading, maybe the sun will be out again," said Chloe.

Chloe began reading short stories about different parts of the world.

"I wish I could travel to some of these places. How fun would that be!" thought Chloe.

As Chloe began reading, she fell into a deep sleep.

"Where am I?" Chloe asked.

"Welcome to Liberia!" said the Griot.

"Where is Liberia?" asked Chloe.

"Liberia is a country on the continent of Africa. It is the first stop in your travels. We will visit one country on each of the seven continents around the world. I am a Griot, an ancient African storyteller. I will be your guide along the way. Please, don't worry! You will be safe," stated the Griot.

"The capital of Liberia is Monrovia. It is the home of Liberia's National Museum. At the museum, you will meet our country's President, Ellen Johnson Sirleaf. She is our country's first elected female Head of State. She will teach you about our culture, food, and history," said the Griot.

Liberia's President:
Ellen Johnson Sirleaf

"Dear Little Brown Girl, have a seat. Let me teach you about Liberia, our language, and what we like to eat.

In Liberia, rice and fish are popular foods to eat. Our native language is English, but we are a multilingual country where more than thirty languages are spoken.

Liberia is off the Atlantic Coast, which is our beach. Drums are also popular here so you can dance to your own beat.

However, I want to encourage you that you can be whatever you want to be!" said President Sirleaf.

"Come on, Chloe! Our second destination is the United Kingdom so you can meet their Prime Minister.

Follow me and Prime Minister Theresa May will explain the British history and language to you in her very own way," shouted the Griot.

"Dear Little Brown Girl, what would you like to know?" asked Prime Minister Theresa May.

"Where is the United Kingdom?" Chloe asked.

"The United Kingdom is on the continent of Europe and is made up of England, Scotland, Wales, and Northern Ireland. Our capital is London and the birthplace of Shakespeare and The Beatles. Shakespeare was a popular playwriter and The Beatles was the best musical group, you might say!

Our official language is English, in which you and I speak. The United Kingdom is quite chic," said Prime Minister Theresa May.

United Kingdom's Prime Minister:

Theresa May

"Would you like some fish & chips?" asked Prime Minister May.

"It's a famous staple here among the people in the UK. Sports and literature are our country's claim to fame. Soccer, rugby, cricket, boxing, and golf were all invented here. Harry Potter was also written in Britain," stated Prime Minister May.

"I was smitten with Britain and the knowledge I learned today. Maybe, I will become a Head of State, one day!" said Chloe.

"Chloe, are you ready for continent number three?" the Griot asked.

We are headed to Bangladesh where you will see many trees!" stated the Griot.

"Can I ask a question?" asked Chloe.

"Yes, of course," confirmed the Griot.

"Where is Bangladesh and who is the Prime Minister there?" Chloe asked.

"Hold tight and you will see! You will meet Prime Minister Sheikh Hasina in 1...2...3!" exclaimed the Griot.

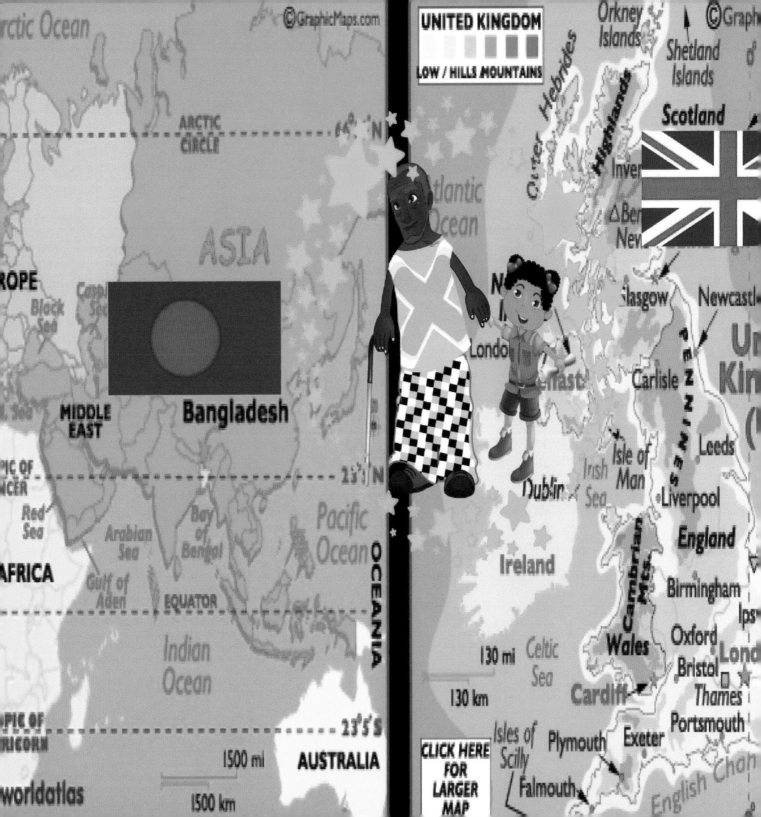

"Dear Little Brown Girl, what would you like to know?" asked Prime Minister Hasina.

"Where is Bangladesh and what will we explore?" Chloe asked.

"We are located on the continent of Asia, where you will see Bengal Tigers and other wild animals run free. Nevertheless, be careful because there is one rule you must follow. Always use your right hand for whatever you must do, the left hand is considered unclean and breaks our cultural rules," stated Prime Minister Hasina.

"Why do the people here look so mean?" asked Chloe.

"The people here seldom smile, it's a sign of immaturity so don't let it get you down. It's a part of our culture, you will learn today, but Bangladesh is a fun place to stay. Our official language is Bengali and you can learn it easily," said Prime Minister Hasina.

Bangladesh's Prime Minister:

Sheikh Hasina

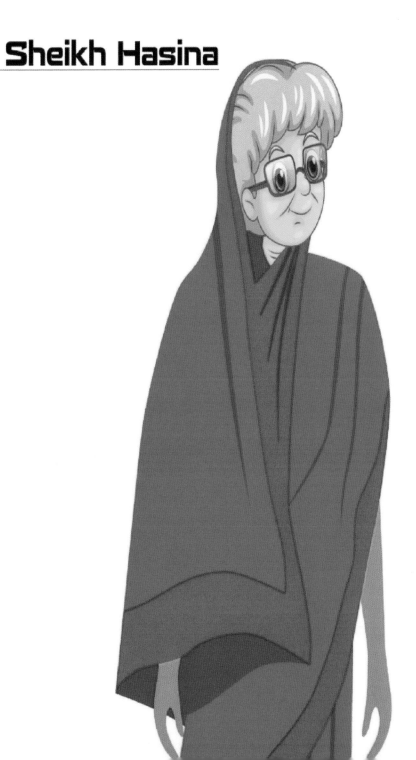

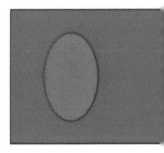

"Unlike most places you will visit around the world, Bangladesh has six seasons and a lot of farmland to explore. One thing you will see is half of our population is farmers that love to plant and sing," announced Prime Minister Hasina.

Bangladesh has the longest unbroken sea beach and sometimes we become flooded out, but our land has never frozen-that's something to smile about!

Bangladesh is a beautiful country to discover, but I want to leave this with you to uncover. You can be anything you want to be, all you have to do is believe," said Prime Minister Hasina.

"Let's move on to continent number four. Hurry, Chloe we have a lot to explore! We have seen Africa, Europe, and Asia. Our next stop is the continent of Australia," proclaimed the Griot.

"I can't wait to see the sea birds flying and meet the first female Prime Minister of Marshall Island," stated Chloe.

"Dear Little Brown Girl, I can't wait to show you around and give you facts about our little town.

I'm the first female President of this island, you know! I am also the first to earn a doctorate degree on Marshall Island. I am passionate about education as you can see because I want all little boys and girls to succeed. Our official language is comprised of two- some people speak English and Marshallese, too," said President Dr. Hilda Heine.

Marshall Island's President:

Dr. Hilda Heine

"One of the highlights of our island is the aquarium that displays different types of fish and Laura Beach Park where visitors can make a wish. Our small islands tie families together into clans and allows family gatherings to expand. First birthday celebrations are significant on Marshall Island, a time where everyone can meet on the highlands!

Dear Little Brown Girl, we celebrate you! You only have a few continents left to view. You can be a Head of State where ever you like to be.

My advice is...don't give up on your dreams", declared Prime Minister Heine.

"Chloe, we only have two more continents to go," said the Griot.

"I thought there were seven continents to explore. We only visited four of seven, so we have three more to see," said Chloe.

"Yes Chloe, you are right, but there is nothing on continent number 5. It will be a sore sight to see. We can skip Antarctica because it's way down South, the Southernmost continent without a doubt! We can go to Antarctica, but you will see a lot of snow. Grab your coat and let's go! There are no permanent people or places to go," said the Griot.

"Chloe, change your clothes and prepare for the tropical weather. Our next destination is continent #6...South America. Oh, what a picturesque place to be! Get ready, Chloe, we are heading to Chile!" said the Griot.

"Dear Little Brown Girl, welcome to Chile! We hope you enjoy your stay. I'm Michelle Bachelet, the President of this country. First, I want to share some facts with you before we grab our maps and head out. I am the first female President to be elected twice, the people here in Chile are very nice," said President Bachelet.

"What will I see?" asked Chloe.

"Please tell me what makes Chile so unique!" stated Chloe.

"Chile has the biggest swimming pool in the world. The pool is over 1,000 yards. You can also visit the Atacama Desert, one of the driest place on Earth or you can surf with the penguins, of course. Dear Little Brown Girl, there's so much to see. Chile has the Andes Mountains where people desire to be. We also have empanadas filled with meat and cheese.

Chile's President:

Michelle Bachelet

Dear Little Brown Girl, one thing before you go. The more you know, the more you can grow! On your travels, back home to North America, be safe. Nothing can separate you but time and space. My advice to you is to seek knowledge while it can be found, so one day you can wear a crown," exclaimed President Michelle Bachelet.

"Chloe, Chloe, we have to get you back home... to continent number #7 where you belong," announced the Griot.

"The United States of America is a country on the continent of North America, where there has not been a female President ever", exclaimed the Griot.

"Chloe, maybe you can run for President in 2030, and be the first female to ever win it! Hillary Clinton was very close, just maybe Chloe, you will win all the votes," stated the Griot.

Suddenly, Chloe woke up out of her sleep and realized she can be President, if she wanted to be. After visiting different countries and speaking to different Heads of States, Chloe knew what she wanted to be one day!

"I want to be the President of the United States (the land of life, liberty, and freedom of speech), a place where I can be me!" declared Chloe.

Just remember you can be whatever you want to be!

97117635R00027

Made in the USA
Columbia, SC
07 June 2018